Dinosaurs and Prehistoric Animals

Megalodon

by Janet Riehecky

Consulting Editor: Gail Saunders-Smith, PhD

Consultant: Jack Horner, Curator of Paleontology
Museum of the Rockies
Bozeman, Montana

Capstone
press

Mankato, Minnesota

Pebble Plus is published by Capstone Press,
1710 Roe Crest Drive, North Mankato, Minnesota 56003.
www.capstonepub.com

Library of Congress Cataloging-in-Publication Data
Riehecky, Janet, 1953–
    Megalodon / by Janet Riehecky.
    p. cm.—(Pebble plus. Dinosaurs and prehistoric animals)
    Summary: "Simple text and illustrations present the life of megalodon, how it looked, and its behavior"—
Provided by publisher.
    Includes bibliographical references and index.
    ISBN-13: 978-0-7368-5354-5 (hardcover)
    ISBN-10: 0-7368-5354-5 (hardcover)
    ISBN-13: 978-0-7368-6911-9 (softcover pbk.)
    ISBN-10: 0-7368-6911-5 (softcover pbk.)
    1. Carcharocles megalodon—Juvenile literature. I. Title. II. Series.
QE852.L35R54 2006
567'.3—dc22   2005020798

Editorial Credits
Sarah L. Schuette, editor; Linda Clavel, designer; Wanda Winch, photo researcher

Illustration and Photo Credits
Jon Hughes, illustrator
Robert S. Dietz Museum of Geology, Arizona State University/Brad Archer, 21

The author dedicates this book to her nephew Matthew.

Note to Parents and Teachers

The Dinosaurs and Prehistoric Animals set supports national science standards related
to the evolution of life. This book describes and illustrates megalodon. The images
support early readers in understanding the text. The repetition of words and phrases
helps early readers learn new words. This book also introduces early readers to
subject-specific vocabulary words, which are defined in the Glossary section. Early
readers may need assistance to read some words and to use the Table of Contents,
Glossary, Read More, Internet Sites, and Index sections of the book.

Printed in the United States of America in North Mankato, Minnesota.
102014
008509R

Table of Contents

megalodon (MEG-uh-lo-don)

A Giant Shark

Megalodon was

a giant prehistoric shark.

Its huge teeth were

as sharp as knives.

Megalodon swam in oceans
around the world.
It lived about 30 million
years ago.

How Megalodon Looked

Megalodon was as long
as a city bus.
It was about 50 feet
(15 meters) long.

Megalodon had fins
on its body and tail.
Fins helped megalodon
swim quickly.

Megalodon had gills.

It used its gills

to breathe underwater.

Megalodon had

a rounded snout.

Its wide jaws

were filled with teeth.

What Megalodon Did

Megalodon searched
the ocean for animals to eat.
It hunted large whales.

Megalodon bit its food
into chunks.
It swallowed
the chunks whole.

The End of Megalodon

Megalodons died

about 2 million years ago.

No one knows why

they all died.

You can see megalodon teeth

in museums.

Glossary

fin—a flap on the body of a fish; megalodons used fins to steer and move through the water.

gill—a breathing organ on the side of a fish

jaw—a set of bones that holds teeth

museum—a place where objects of art, history, or science are shown

prehistoric—very, very old; prehistoric means belonging to a time before history was written down.

snout—the long part of a megalodon's face that includes its nose, mouth, and jaws

teeth—the sharp, bony parts of a megalodon's mouth; scientists have found fossils of megalodon teeth.

Read More

Arnold, Caroline. *Giant Shark: Megalodon, Prehistoric Super Predator.* New York: Clarion, 2000.

O'Brien, Patrick. *Megatooth.* New York: Henry Holt, 2001.

Taylor, L. R. *Great White Sharks.* Early Bird Nature Books. Minneapolis: Lerner, 2006.

Internet Sites

FactHound offers a safe, fun way to find Internet sites related to this book. All of the sites on FactHound have been researched by our staff.

Here's how:

1. Visit *www.facthound.com*

2. Type in this special code **0736853545** for age-appropriate sites. Or enter a search word related to this book for a more general search.

3. Click on the **Fetch It** button.

FactHound will fetch the best sites for you!

Index

Word Count: 123
Grade: 1
Early-Intervention Level: 12